The Story of
HANUKKAH

by Norma Simon
illustrated by Leonid Gore

HarperCollins*Publishers*

For my cousins Ruth and Jud
with much love
—N. S.

For Danny
—L. G.

The illustrations in this book were done using a mixed media technique with ink and acrylic.

The text for this book was first published in *Hanukkah*, a Crowell Holiday Book edited by Susan Bartlett Weber, written by Norma Simon and illustrated by Symeon Shimin in 1966. • Text copyright © 1966 by Norma Simon • Copyright renewed 1994 by Norma Simon • Illustrations copyright © 1997 by Leonid Gore • Printed in the U.S.A. All rights reserved. • Library of Congress Cataloging-in-Publication Data• Visit us on the World Wide Web! http://www.harperchildrens.com • Simon, Norma. • The story of Hanukkah / by Norma Simon ; illustrated by Leonid Gore. p. cm. • Summary: Explains the history and traditions that are a part of the Jewish holiday of Hanukkah. • ISBN 0-06-027419-0. — ISBN 0-06-027420-4 (lib. bdg.) — ISBN 0-06-443511-3 (pbk.) • I. Hanukkah—Juvenile literature. [I. Hanukkah.] I. Gore, Leonid, ill. II. Title. • BM695.H3S53 1997 296.4'35—dc20 96-5141 CIP AC • Typography by Elynn Cohen • Newly Illustrated Edition

❖

The Story of
HANUKKAH

E ACH WINTER, all over the world, Jewish families polish the Hanukkah menorah until it gleams. Now is the time to prepare for the Festival of Lights.

Hanukkah begins on the eve of the twenty-fifth day of the Hebrew month Kislev. This day falls at the end of November or sometime during December.

Jewish children love the menorah, with its small candles that burn during the eight nights of Hanukkah. The bright lights remind them of the Jews' fight to worship God in their own way.

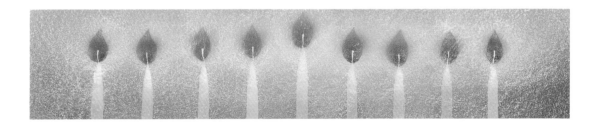

The story of Hanukkah begins more than two thousand years ago in a land called Judea, nestled between the Mediterranean Sea and the Dead Sea. There the Jewish people lived and worked.

At that time Antiochus of Syria, a neighboring state, ruled Judea. He wanted the Jewish people to pray to the Greek gods, as he did. But the Jews had prayed to one God for over a thousand years, from the time of Moses, and they refused.

Antiochus decided to punish them. He said they would be put to death unless they gave up their Jewish religion.

Antiochus sent his soldiers to the villages and cities. They burned the Jewish holy books and ordered the Jews to pray to statues of the Greek gods. They placed a huge statue of the Greek god Zeus in the Jewish Temple in Jerusalem, the capital of Judea.

Some Jews were persuaded to give up their religion. But most Jews were prepared to die if they could not pray to one God. They could not forget the ways their ancestors had taught them.

The Jewish people were in grave danger and in great need of help. Then one day a leader appeared. He was an old Jewish priest named Mattathias, who lived with his five sons in the village of Modin, northwest of Jerusalem.

When the king's soldiers marched into Modin, they ordered Mattathias to pray to the Greek gods. The bearded priest shouted, "No!"

But one of the fearful villagers stepped forward and said, "I will pray to the Greek gods."

Mattathias turned red with anger over the man's betrayal. He seized a sword and killed the Jewish traitor and one of the king's soldiers.

Mattathias gathered his people around him. "Whosoever is for God, let him follow me!" he commanded.

Mattathias and his sons quickly fled Modin and hid in caves in the mountains. Many other villagers left their homes to join the Jewish fighters.

Mattathias was the leader of this small band of brave men for many years. Whenever they could, they fought against the Syrian soldiers. Finally, Mattathias grew too old to fight, and his son Judah took his place.

Judah and his followers were called the Maccabees. Maccabee means "hammer" in Hebrew, the language of the Jews.

Jews from every part of Judea joined the Maccabees. But even so, there were far more Syrian soldiers. Judah Maccabee had to be a wise and clever general. He led his army in surprise nighttime attacks. Before the enemy could strike back, the Maccabees disappeared into the hills.

The Jewish army grew tired from the long years of warfare, but they continued to fight and won many strategic battles because they knew the land so well. But all weariness was forgotten on the triumphant day they captured Jerusalem from the Syrians.

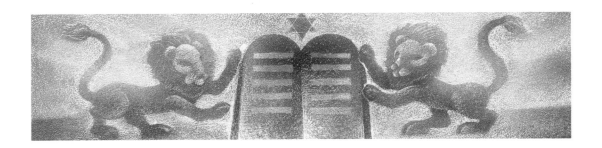

Judah and his army destroyed the many statues of the Greek gods in the Temple. Then they carefully made the Temple a house of prayer to one God again.

When the Temple was ready, the Jews celebrated their victory and the rededication of the Temple for eight days. All the people proclaimed that this celebration should be held each year.

So from that time forward, a holiday was celebrated with joy and gladness for eight days, beginning on the twenty-fifth of Kislev. Later, this holiday was given the name Hanukkah, which means "dedication" in Hebrew. The story of Judah and his army became a part of the history of the Jews.

Much later a legend grew to be part of the Hanukkah story, too.

On that first Hanukkah, the legend says, the priests wanted to light the Temple menorah. The menorah's flame would remind them that God was with them. They looked for jars of olive oil to burn in the menorah but found only one small jar with enough pure oil for one day. It would take eight days to make new oil. There seemed to be nothing they could do.

So the precious oil was poured into the menorah. It should not have burned for more than one day, but on the second day the flame still shone. It shone on the third day. And on the fourth. Each day the oil kept burning. On the eighth day, when the new oil was ready, the menorah was still bright with light. It seemed like a miracle.

In ancient times most menorahs had seven branches. But the Hanukkah menorahs we light today have one center branch and eight side branches to remind us of the miracle of the oil that lasted eight days.

The sons of Mattathias were leaders of the Jews the rest of their lives. As the years passed, Jewish families scattered to other lands near Judea. Still later, some of them settled in Eastern Europe, in what are now Poland, Russia, Hungary, and Rumania. Wherever they went, they carried their religion to their new homes. Every year, their children and their children's children celebrated the festival of Hanukkah.

Many of the Jews in the United States and Canada today come from families who once lived in Eastern Europe. Among the things their families brought to the New World were beautiful Hanukkah menorahs. These menorahs burned oil in small cups. Now most menorahs hold thin wax candles. They are made of wood, brass, copper, or silver. A few are made of gold.

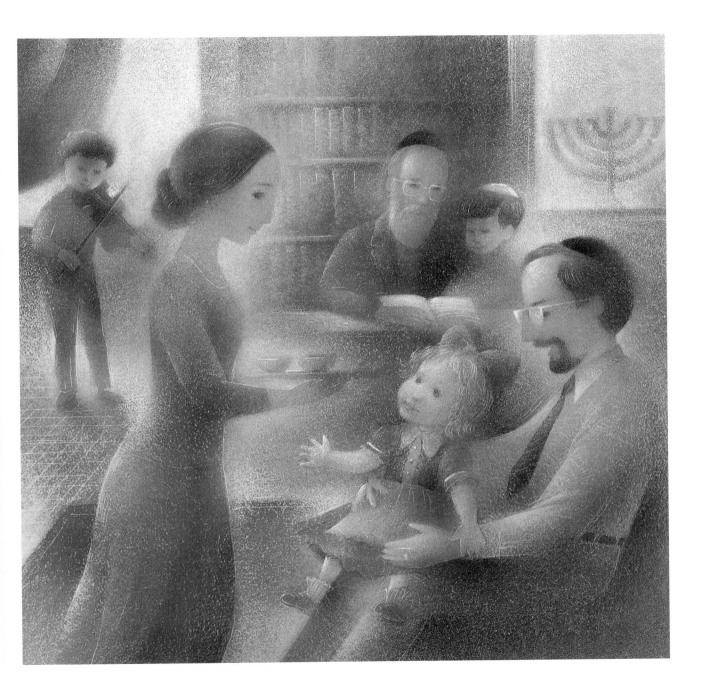

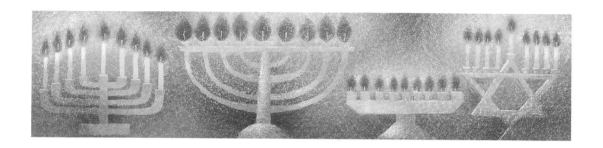

In traditional Jewish homes the eight nights of Hanukkah begin with the lighting of the menorah. The menorah holds nine candles. Eight of the candles stand for the eight days the oil burned in the legend of the first Hanukkah. The ninth is different. It is the shammash candle. Shammash means "servant" in Hebrew.

Each night the shammash is lit first. Then it is used to light the other candles. One more candle is lit each night. The menorah burns brighter and brighter. The family recites blessings in Hebrew or in English. One blessing is: "Blessed are you, O Lord our God, who did wondrous things for our ancestors long ago at this time of year."

Every night the lighted menorah is placed on the windowsill so that all who pass may see the burning candles and remember the miracle of Hanukkah.

During the holidays pounds of potatoes are grated for making latkes, or potato pancakes. Eating latkes with sour cream or apple-sauce is an old Hanukkah custom.

Every night after supper comes a time for storytelling and games. The children listen to the exciting story of Hanukkah. They also play a very old game, spin the dreidel.

The dreidel is a top. Once dreidels were made of lead, but today they are usually made of wood or plastic. A dreidel always has four sides. On each side is one Hebrew letter: Nun, or נ; Gimmel, or ג; Hay, or ה; Shin, or ש. These are the first letters of the Hebrew words "Nes Gadol Hayah Sham," which means: "A great miracle happened there."

Neighbors and relatives come to visit. They tell stories about other family Hanukkahs. Young and old voices join in the singing of "Ma'oz Tsur," a Hebrew hymn that tells of the bravery of the Jews.

Many children go to Hanukkah parties at their synagogues. They sing holiday songs in Hebrew, Yiddish, and English. They put on plays and act out the ancient story of the Jews' courageous fight to pray to their own God. Judah Maccabee is always the hero, and Antiochus is the villain.

Gifts of gelt, or money, are an old custom, too. The night the first candle is lighted, Hanukkah gelt is given to the children. Some parents give a small gift each evening.

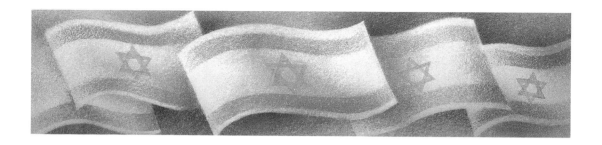

Judea, the old land of the Maccabees, is now part of the land we call Israel. It is the homeland of the Jews again, and Hebrew is the national language.

In Israel, during Hanukkah, huge menorahs are lit. They shine from high watchtowers, synagogues, and the tops of city halls.

People travel to Modin, the town of the Maccabees. They visit caves where the Jewish soldiers hid many centuries ago.

Like the Maccabees, most people want the right to pray to God in their own way. This right is called freedom of religion.

The spirit of Hanukkah, the Festival of Lights, is shared by all people who love freedom.

Things to Make and Do During Hanukkah

The Dreidel Game

A dreidel is a four-sided top with a Hebrew letter on each side. The letters are Nun, Gimmel, Hay, and Shin, which stand for the phrase "Nes Gadol Haya Sham," or "A Great Miracle Happened There." In Israel dreidels have the letters Nun, Gimmel, Hay, and Peh, which stand for "A Great Miracle Happened *Here.*"

Any number of people can play the dreidel game. Each player starts with ten pieces of Hanukkah gelt. You can use anything for the gelt— pennies, nuts, candies.

To begin, each player puts one piece of gelt into the "pot," or in the center of the table. Then the first player spins the dreidel.

When the dreidel lands, if the letter facing up is

Nun   נ   the player does nothing and the next player takes a turn.

Gimmel   ג   the player takes all of the gelt in the pot. Each player again contributes one piece of gelt to the pot and the next player takes a turn.

Hay   ה   the player takes half of the gelt in the pot and the next player takes a turn. (If there is an odd number of pieces of gelt in the pot, the player may take the extra piece.)

Shin   שׁ   the player puts one piece of gelt into the pot, and the next player takes a turn.

The game ends when one player has won all of the gelt. Or you could limit the game to a certain amount of time. When the time is up, the player with the most gelt is the winner.

Potato Latkes

No one is sure how latkes became a traditional part of the Hanukkah celebration, but they are fried in oil, which perhaps symbolizes the miracle of the oil. In Israel jelly doughnuts fried in oil are a popular treat during Hanukkah. Ask an adult to help you make these delicious potato pancakes. Hot oil and batter can spit and spatter. Watch out, please!

Ingredients:

4 large Idaho or russet potatoes
(about 2 pounds)
1 small onion
2 eggs, lightly beaten

$\frac{1}{3}$ cup flour (or matzoh meal)
1 teaspoon salt
$\frac{1}{4}$ teaspoon baking powder
oil for frying

Wash the potatoes well and then grate them, skins and all, with a vegetable grater or in a food processor. Put the grated potatoes in a colander and suspend the colander over a large bowl or place it in the sink so the potato water can drain off.

Peel the onion, trim off the ends, and grate it. In a large bowl, mix together the beaten eggs, the flour (or matzoh meal), the salt, and the baking powder. Add the grated onion and the drained, grated potatoes and stir well.

Place a large frying pan over medium-high heat. Add enough oil to cover the bottom of the pan. The oil is hot enough to cook latkes when a small piece of bread dropped into the oil sizzles and turns brown. Using a tablespoon, scoop up some potato batter and gently drop it into the oil. Cook the latkes, a few at a time, until they are crisp and golden brown—about 2 or 3 minutes on each side.

Place finished latkes on a baking sheet lined with paper towels and keep them warm in a 300° oven until all the batter is used up. This recipe makes enough for 4 to 6 people.

Serve the latkes with applesauce or sour cream or both. Enjoy!

The Hebrew Calendar

The Hebrew calendar has twelve months, each month lasting 29 or 30 days. The Jewish New Year, Rosh Hashanah, is celebrated in the month of Tishre, which usually falls in the English month of September or October. Listed below are the Hebrew months, the Hebrew dates for the holidays, the names of the holidays, and the corresponding English months.

Tishre	1–2, Rosh Hashanah	September–October
	10, Yom Kippur	
	15–22, Sukkot	
	23, Simhat Torah	
Heshvan	—	October–November
Kislev	25, Hanukkah	November–December
Tevet	—	December–January
Shevat	15, Tu B'Shevat	January–February
Adar	14, Purim	February–March
Nisan	15–22, Passover	March–April
	27, Yom Hashoah	
Iyar	5, Yom Ha'Atzma'Ut	April–May
Sivan	6–7, Shavuot	May–June
Tammuz	—	June–July
Av	—	July–August
Elul	—	August–September

Happy holidays! Happy Hanukkah!